LOUISE NEVELSON

LOUISE NEVELSON

PRINTS AND DRAWINGS

1953-1966

LOUISE NEVELSON
Photograph by Diana MacKown

Designed, printed and distributed for The Brooklyn Museum
by Shorewood Publishers, Inc., New York City

Text by

UNA E. JOHNSON

Curator of Prints and Drawings
The Brooklyn Museum

Research by

JO MILLER

Assistant Curator of Prints and Drawings
The Brooklyn Museum

Monograph No. 5 in the series:

AMERICAN GRAPHIC ARTISTS OF THE TWENTIETH CENTURY

published by The Brooklyn Museum under a grant from
The Ford Foundation Program in Humanities and the Arts

ACKNOWLEDGMENTS

Special acknowledgments are made to Louise Nevelson and her assistant, Diana MacKown, who made prints available for research; to Irwin Hollander of the Hollander Graphic Workshop, and to Mrs. Colette Roberts, Tamarind Lithography Workshop, and Pace Gallery. Special thanks are extended to Mr. Thomas B. Hess and *Art News* magazine for permission to reprint the untitled poem by Mrs. Nevelson.

INTRODUCTION

LOUISE NEVELSON'S prints and drawings may best be viewed in conjunction with the rich imagery and lively immediacy of her sculpture. Thus are the total magnitude of her creative powers and their productive results brought into full realization. As an artist she commands a flood tide of ideas and the enormous energy and enthusiasm with which to carry them to completion. At the height of her career Nevelson has summed up the development of her visual ideas and experiences: "I first wanted to give structure to shadow—now I want to give structure to reflection."

Born in Kiev, Russia in 1900, Louise Nevelson moved with her family to Rockland, Maine in 1905 and very early decided that she would be an artist. In 1929, she studied with Kenneth Hayes Miller at the Art Students League in New York and in 1931 she went to Munich to study with Hans Hofmann. In both Munich and Vienna she was given parts in various modern film productions and also worked with modern dance groups. In 1941 she held her first one-man exhibition of sculpture at the Nierendorf Gallery in New York. Long interested in pre-Columbian art, she made several extended archeological trips to Mexico and South America during 1948–49.

While on her journeys in Mexico, Central America and South America, she was greatly impressed by the sculpture and the profusion of sculptural reliefs on the great Mayan temples. The drama of wild landscapes in which the ever-present jungle ceaselessly encroached upon the symbols of a remote and sophisticated civilization appealed to her own active imagination. These images and symbols caused Nevelson to observe: "This was a world of forms that at once I felt I could identify with, a world where East and West met, a world of geometry and magic." There followed the artist's series of black terracotta figures. In them the subtle relationships of forms merged with the underlying abstract elements of the total composition. Incised lines suggested a face, a gesture or a fleeting attitude and gave to the sculptural forms a graphic delineation. Her very titles—*The Night Bishop, Game Figure,* and *The Clown with the World in the Palm of His Hand* (the latter cast in bronze)—carry out a continuing dialogue of ideas at once poetic and occasionally caustically witty. Similar ideas and figures were to appear in her later wood sculptures and the etchings of 1953–55.

Earlier in the mid-1940's Louise Nevelson had visited Atelier 17 in New York where, under the aegis of Stanley William Hayter, a group of internationally known artists were gathered to explore and to initiate new aspects of the old art of printmaking. However, it was not until 1953 that Nevelson actually began to work at Atelier 17 on her first series of intaglio prints. Hayter himself had already returned to Paris, leaving the direction of the studio to several artists who were familiar with its routine.

The formal techniques of printmaking were of little consequence to Nevelson. Instead her over-riding desire was to find a means whereby an artist of her intuitive powers could seize and exploit selected elements emanating from the unpremeditated images. Nevelson sought a new means of expanding the many ideas and forms that were already beginning to appear in her sculptures. Thus the etchings *Ancient City, The King and Queen,* and *Jungle Figures* became the immediate forerunners of the magic webs of rectangles that make up her elongated totems and sculptured walls.

The creative excitement generated by these plastic forms was channelled not into the development of a technique or style but into constructed forms that heralded a different if not new idiom. These were dark images of Byzantine richness and splendor set within a Gothic intensity. Nevelson's exploitation of symbolic forms was similar to that employed by surrealist artists earlier in the century. However she never allowed a style to dominate or to interfere with her ideas. Along with Alexander Calder and David Smith, Nevelson may be considered one of those important American artists who are superb innovators of new sculptural forms. Nevelson has elaborated: "Architecture is everywhere order is. There is architecture about our bodies, about the things we build and it does not have to be a house."

Louise Nevelson's prints fall within three productive periods of concentrated work. The first series, completed between 1953 and 1955, was restricted to etching and variations within this particular medium. Her preparation of the copper plate was unconventional and followed no prescribed rules. Often while the plate was reposing in the acid bath the artist worked on it with any available or likely tool at hand, thus disturbing or reaccenting the etch. The prints appear deeply etched and darkly inked, with the resulting effect not unlike that of her black sculptures. Strange landscapes float in the murky textures and mysterious forms that crowd her compositions. Never caught within the small technical eddies of her media Nevelson pursues what has been termed "a nostalgic Elsewhere."

Her first one-man exhibition of etchings, under the special title of "Moon-scapes," was held at the Lotte Jacobi Gallery in New York in 1954. It was not until the second showing of her etchings, held in conjunction with her large sculptural walls at Grand Central Moderns early in 1955, that her intaglio prints came into logical focus. Here the handling of spatial ideas came under the discipline of a two-dimensional surface. It is to be remembered that Nevelson had studied with Hans Hofmann at the Academy in Munich in the fall and winter of 1931. Hofmann's penetration of the new visual elements in space through the breaking up of abstract forms appealed to Nevelson with her predilection for unpremeditated visual exploration. Nevelson's approach to printmaking was that of changing or disturbing the surface of her vehicle of expression through the seizure of an intuitive form or idea and exploiting it with concentrated energy and purpose. The early etching entitled *The Sunken Cathedral* seems to rise from the mists of an "elsewhere" landscape. The different tensions created by breaking up an existing surface and suggesting a third dimension are to be noted in *Ancient City, The Search* and the more simplified *Mirrored Figure*. The latter etching is composed of five rectangular forms with lightly designated figures. The composition is tentative and experimental rather than a complete statement.

The West Queen, The Stone Figures that Walk in the Night and *Ancient Sculpture Garden* are perhaps Nevelson's tribute to the great sculptural heritage of Mexico and Central America sifted through her own vision. In the prints *The King and Queen* and *Solid Reflections,* the ideas and forms become a single unit of expression. The figures, highlighted against the undefined mystery of space, are held within a moment of time. Nevelson considers them voyages or explorations into an "elsewhere" achieved through a visible spectrum of illusive figures. In the descriptive lines of an untitled poem the artist continues to search for and capture other expressive forms and abstract ideas.

> Queen of the black black
> In the valley of all all
> With one glance sees the King.
> Mountain top
> The Climb
> The Way
> Restless Winds
> Midnight blooms
> Tons of colors

Tones of waterdrops
Crystal reflections
Painting mirages.
Celestial splendor.
Highest grandeur
Queen of the black black.
King of the all all*

It was some ten years later, in 1963, that Nevelson carried out the second period of her graphic work. During this time she completed twenty-six large-scale lithographs—nineteen in black and white and seven in black and white and a single color. She spent six weeks working with her usual intensity at the Tamarind Lithography Workshop in Los Angeles where, with able professional assistance, she explored the intricate nuances of lithography. She found this a most sympathetic medium in tune with her tremendous creative energy and responsive to her highly intuitive method of working. Her lithographs, all untitled, are free from the sculptural forms that often dominate her earlier intaglio work. The most abstract and perhaps the most powerful of her entire graphic works, these lithographs chart a shadowy world of reflections. They are great night landscapes with clusters of glittering lights and piercing white lines that stab into the depths of space. Here appear lacy patterns and sudden visions seen from great heights.

The perceptive observer may find in these large, mysterious black-and-white visions something of the strange fantasies of Poe and the vivid imagery that floods the poetry of Whitman. Such expressions record a willingness, in fact a determination, to create a new idiom and to venture into different interpretations of an art form.

As in her earlier intaglio work, Nevelson's handling of the lithographic medium is also unconventional. She may draw freely and directly upon the prepared stone or zinc plate with crayon and washes or indirectly onto transfer paper which is then cut into free forms and impressed on the stone. She also may achieve special textures through the use of lace or coarse textiles pressed on the prepared stone under washes of tusche in order to obtain heightened contrasts. On occasion, she may produce shadowy grays for greater spatial effects through the application of hard erasers directly on the stone itself. Her inventiveness and her ability to

*Reprinted from *Art News,* September, 1961

work around the clock taxed even the splendid capabilities of the well-organized Tamarind Lithography Workshop.

The third period of her involvement with the printed image began late in 1965 at Irwin Hollander's Graphic Workshop in New York. There in a single day she completed eight etched plates, of which *Totem's Presents* is the most outstanding example. At the same time, she selected a group of her 1953-55 etching plates which were then printed by Emiliano Sironi under the supervision of the artist. These editions were printed on heavy Rives paper. A few impressions of earlier designated editions were printed from the plates by the artist but were never completed.

Several new lithographs also were issued in very small editions during this third period of work. Perhaps the lithographs of the preceding period at Tamarind and the two latest ones printed at Hollander's shop, entitled *Dawnlight* and *Innerview*, constitute her strongest and most fully realized graphic work to date. They stand as independent statements and are no longer reminiscent of her sculptural forms.

While Nevelson is a deft and unpredictable innovator, she is also a highly disciplined artist cognizant of the classic tradition in art. This discipline is readily seen in her drawings. She has made hundreds of pen and pencil line drawings of classic simplicity and directness. Entirely figurative, they form a never-ending diary carried out in a personal calligraphy. Perhaps as a respite from her larger abstract sculptures, they are a continuing series of standing and seated nude figures and a number of smaller portrait heads, each delineated in free and flowing lines. Others are built up through an endless maze of wiry lines but still are held within the basic outline of the human figure. This pulsating visual recording of spinning forms may suddenly be arrested and channelled into an eloquent and spare economy of statement, as in the composition entitled *Archaic Head.* Here the cadence and rhythm of a single flowing form are held strictly within the discipline of a lean, sure line. Still another pencil drawing, *Seated Female Figure,* captures a poignant memory of Mayan sculpture in the suggested blockiness of the composition and in the repose of the figure itself. Such drawings of the figure are set down on the sheet of paper with commanding ease and assurance.

Nevelson, as other artists of her generation, has not forgotten the discouraging years of the 1930's and the abysmal lack of recognition and meagre financial remuneration that were the lot of the more creative artists in the United States. While Nevelson enjoys her present international acclaim and affluence, she also remembers that both have come very late in a long and dedicated career. An understandable bitterness has made her gravely critical but in no way has it been reflected in her work. She has observed with both wit and seriousness: "If you want an empire, dear, you have to build it." This is in reference not to a personal domain but to the far different realm of creative ideas, insights and reflections. These she has built into sculptural and graphic forms through the challenges of a personal style and the changing images of her own time. With characteristic directness Nevelson frankly states: "I wish to own my time and to claim it." She explains further: "My total conscious search in life has been for a new seeing, a new image, a new insight. This search not only includes the object, but the in-between places, the dawns and the dusks, the objective world, the heavenly spheres, the places between the land and the sea. Whatever creation man invents, the image can be found in nature. We cannot see anything of which we are not already aware. The inner and the outer equal one."

UNA E. JOHNSON

CATALOGUE

NOTES ON THE CATALOGUE

Dimensions are listed in inches with height preceding width. Measurements given for intaglio prints are those of the plate mark; sheet size is given for lithographs. The formal editions from the intaglio plates were printed on French Rives BFK paper by Emiliano Sironi under the supervision of Irwin Hollander at the Hollander Graphic Workshop in New York City in 1965 and 1966. Each impression bears the embossed printer's chop ES in the lower right margin. The editions are numbered and signed by the artist in pencil in the lower right margin. Artist's proofs of the editions are in the collection of The Brooklyn Museum and were a gift of the artist in memory of Theodore Haseltine. In 1963, a series of lithographs was printed at Tamarind Lithography Workshop in Los Angeles. The lithographs are signed in pencil in the lower right margin and each impression bears the Tamarind dry stamp and the chop of the printer.

In 1966, two lithographs were printed by Irwin Hollander at the Hollander Graphic Workshop in New York. The editions are numbered and signed in pencil by the artist in the lower right margin. Four artist's proofs were printed with each edition.

PRINTS

1953–1955

. ANCIENT CITY
Etching and drypoint, 13⅝ x 20¾
Edition: 20

2. ANCIENT SCULPTURE
   GARDEN
Etching, 14⅝ x 17¾
Edition: 20
Note: Edition of 20 (incomplete)
entitled *Wild Jungle* printed by
the artist on various papers at
Atelier 17, New York

3. ARCHAIC FIGURE
Etching, 27¼ x 21⅞
Edition: 20
Note: Edition of 30 (incomplete)
entitled *Ancient Figure* printed
by the artist on various papers at
Atelier 17, New York

4. CIRCUS WAGON
Etching, 14⅝ x 17¾
Edition: 20
Note: Early proofs exist under the
same title, printed by the artist on
various papers at Atelier 17, New
York. An unknown number of
impressions are hand-colored by
the artist

5. DANCING FIGURE
Etching and drypoint, 20¾ x 13⅝
Edition: 20
Note: Edition of 20 (incomplete)
entitled *Figure at Mid Noon*
printed by the artist on various
papers at Atelier 17, New York

6. EAST LANDSCAPE
Etching, 13⅝ x 20¾
Edition: 20

7. FLOWER QUEEN
Etching, 19⅞ x 15½
Edition: 20
Note: An unknown number of
hand-colored impressions exist
entitled *Ancient Figure,* printed
by the artist at Atelier 17,
New York

8. GODDESS FROM THE GREAT
   BEYOND
Etching and aquatint, 13½ x 8
Edition: 20
Note: An unknown number of
hand-colored impressions exist
entitled *Figure Four Thousand,*
printed by the artist at Atelier 17,
New York

9. GODDESS ONE
Etching and drypoint, 17¼ x 7
Edition: 20
Note: An unknown number of
impressions exist entitled *Moon
Goddess,* printed by the artist at
Atelier 17, New York, in 1953

10. JUNGLE FIGURES
Etching, 23½ x 19⅞
Edition: 20
Note: Earlier proofs exist entitled
Night Figures, printed by the
artist on various papers at Atelier
17, New York

11. THE KING AND QUEEN
Etching, 21¾ x 27¼
Edition: 20

12. MAGIC GARDEN
Etching, 5⅞ x 8⅝
Edition: 20

13. THE MAGIC GARDEN IN SEA
    LAND
Etching, 14¾ x 16⅜
Edition: 20

14. THE MAGIC GARDEN IN SEA
    LAND, A.
Etching and drypoint, 14¾ x 16¼
Edition: 20
First State: Before drypoint. An
    unknown number of artist's proofs
    exist entitled *Far Away Land-
    scape*, printed by the artist at
    Atelier 17, New York
Second State: The artist turned the
    plate completely around and
    reworked the surface with
    drypoint

15. MAGNIFICENT JUNGLE CATS
Etching, 11⅞ x 13⅝
Edition: 20
Note: Incomplete edition entitled
    Animal Kingdom printed by the
    artist on various papers at
    Atelier 17, New York

16. MIRRORED FIGURE
Etching and drypoint, 7⅜ x 17⅛
Edition: 20
Note: Artist's edition of 20
    (incomplete) entitled *Archaic
    Figures* printed at Atelier 17,
    New York

17. MOON LADY
Etching, 17½ x 21⅞
Edition: 20
Note: Edition of 20 (incomplete)

entitled *The Face in the Moon*
printed by the artist on various
papers at Atelier 17, New York

18. NIGHT GARDEN
Etching, 14⅝ x 17¾
Edition: 20
Note: Unknown number of
    impressions exist entitled *The
    Ancient Garden,* printed by the
    artist at Atelier 17, New York

19. NOBLE LADY
Etching, 19¾ x 15½
Edition: 20
Note: Unknown number of artist's
    proofs entitled *Portrait* printed
    by the artist on various papers
    at Atelier 17, New York

20. ONE ANCIENT FIGURE
Etching, 17½ x 19¾
Edition: 20

21. PORTRAITS
Etching, 19¾ x 23¼
Edition: 20
Note: Edition of 20 (incomplete)
    entitled *Royalty* printed by the
    artist at Atelier 17, New York

22. THE SEARCH
Etching, 21¾ x 17⅝
Edition: 20
Note: Edition of 30 (incomplete)
    entitled *Majesty* printed by the
    artist on various papers at
    Atelier 17, New York

23. THE SILENT ONE
Etching and drypoint, 20⅞ x 13⅝
Edition: 20
Note: Edition of 30 (incomplete)
    entitled *Ancient Figure* printed
    by the artist on various papers at
    Atelier 17, New York

24. SOLID REFLECTIONS
Etching, 27¼ x 21⅞
Edition: 20
First State: Before soft-ground
   texture was added to the figures.
   Edition of 20 (incomplete)
   entitled *In the Jungle* or *The
   Ancient Garden* printed by the
   artist on various papers at
   Atelier 17, New York
Second State: Soft-ground texture
   added to figures

25. STAR GARDEN
Etching, 15½ x 19¾
Edition: 20
Note: Unknown number of
   impressions entitled *Jungle
   Figures II* printed by the artist
   at Atelier 17, New York

26. THE STONE FIGURES THAT
   WALK IN THE NIGHT
Etching and drypoint, 18½ x 18¾
Edition: 20
Note: Earlier proofs exist entitled
   The Colored Jungle and *In the
   Land Where the Trees Talk,*
   printed by the artist on various
   papers at Atelier 17, New York

27. THE SUNKEN CATHEDRAL
Etching and drypoint, 20¾ x 13⅝
Edition: 20
Note: Early proofs exist printed by
   the artist at Atelier 17, New York

28. TREES
Etching and drypoint, 13¾ x 20¾
Edition: 20

29. TREES IN CIRCLE
Etching and drypoint, 19¾ x 23½
Edition: 20
Note: Artist's proofs entitled *Trees*
   printed by the artist on various
   papers at Atelier 17, New York

30. THE WEST QUEEN
Etching and drypoint, 20¾ x 13⅝
Edition: 20
Note: Edition of 30 (incomplete)
   entitled *Figure* printed by the
   artist on various papers at
   Atelier 17, New York

1963

31. UNTITLED (Tamarind No. 793)
Lithograph in red and black,
   18¾ x 20½
Edition: 20; 2 printer's proofs, 1
   artist's proof, 9 Tamarind
   impressions, 1 presentation proof
Printer: Jason Leese
Note: Printed from one stone and
   one zinc plate

32. UNTITLED (Tamarind No. 794)
Lithograph, 34 x 23½
Edition: 20; 2 printer's proofs, 1
   artist's proof, 9 Tamarind
   impressions, 2 presentation proofs
Printer: Jason Leese

33. UNTITLED (Tamarind No. 795)
Lithograph in black and sanguine,
   32½ x 23¼
Edition: 20; 2 printer's proofs,
   3 artist's proofs, 9 Tamarind
   impressions
Printer: John Dowell, Jr.
Note: Printed from one stone and
   one zinc plate

34. UNTITLED (Tamarind No. 798)
Lithograph, 32 x 22½
Edition: 20; 2 printer's proofs,
   1 artist's proof, 9 Tamarind
   impressions
Printer: Aris Koutroulis

35. UNTITLED (Tamarind No. 799)
Lithograph, 32 x 22
Edition: 20; 2 printer's proofs,
3 artist's proofs, 9 Tamarind
impressions, 1 presentation proof
Printer: Jason Leese

36. UNTITLED (Tamarind No. 801)
Lithograph, 31¼ x 23
Edition: 20; 2 printer's proofs,
1 trial proof, 3 artist's proofs,
9 Tamarind impressions
Printer: John Dowell, Jr.

37. UNTITLED (Tamarind No. 802)
Lithograph, 31½ x 32½
Edition: 20; 2 printer's proofs, 3
artist's proofs, 9 Tamarind
impressions, 1 presentation proof
Printer: Jason Leese

38. UNTITLED (Tamarind No. 805)
Lithograph, 11 x 15¼
Edition: 20; 2 printer's proofs, 2
artist's proofs, 9 Tamarind
impressions
Printer: Aris Koutroulis

39. UNTITLED (Tamarind No. 806)
Lithograph, 38 x 26½
Edition: 20; 2 printer's proofs, 2
artist's proofs, 9 Tamarind
impressions, 1 presentation proof
Printer: Jason Leese

40. UNTITLED (Tamarind No. 808)
Lithograph in brown and black,
11 x 15¼
Edition: 20; 2 printer's proofs, 2
artist's proofs, 9 Tamarind
impressions
Printer: Aris Koutroulis
Note: Printed from one stone and
one zinc plate

41. UNTITLED (Tamarind No. 812)
Lithograph, 32½ x 23
Edition: 20; 2 printer's proofs, 3
artist's proofs, 9 Tamarind
impressions, 1 presentation proof
Printer: John Dowell, Jr.

42. UNTITLED (Tamarind No. 814)
Lithograph, 28½ x 20
Edition: 20; 2 printer's proofs, 2
trial proofs, 2 artist's proofs, 9
Tamarind impressions
Printer: Irwin Hollander

43. UNTITLED (Tamarind No. 816)
Transfer lithograph, 25 x 35
Edition: 20; 2 printer's proofs, 1
artist's proof, 9 Tamarind
impressions
Printer: John Dowell, Jr.

44. UNTITLED (Tamarind No. 817)
Lithograph, 35 x 20
Edition: 20; 2 printer's proofs, 3
artist's proofs, 9 Tamarind
impressions
Printer: Jason Leese

45. UNTITLED (Tamarind No. 820)
Lithograph, 31½ x 22
Edition: 20; 2 printer's proofs, 3
artist's proofs, 9 Tamarind
impressions
Printer: John Dowell, Jr.

46. UNTITLED (Tamarind No. 821)
Lithograph in black and blue,
33 x 23
Edition: 20; 2 printer's proofs, 1
trial proof, 2 artist's proofs, 9
Tamarind impressions
Printer: Irwin Hollander
Note: Printed from one stone and
one zinc plate

47. UNTITLED (Tamarind No. 822)
Lithograph, 10 x 16½
Edition: 20; 2 printer's proofs, 1
artist's proof, 9 Tamarind
impressions, 1 presentation proof
Printer: Aris Koutroulis

48. UNTITLED (Tamarind No. 823)
Transfer lithograph, 30 x 22
Edition: 20; 2 printer's proofs, 1
trial proof, 3 artist's proofs, 9
Tamarind impressions
Printer: John Dowell, Jr.

49. UNTITLED (Tamarind No. 824)
Lithograph, 7¾ x 17½
Edition: 20; 2 printer's proofs, 3
artist's proofs, 9 Tamarind
impressions
Printer: Aris Koutroulis

50. UNTITLED (Tamarind No. 826)
Transfer lithograph, 36 x 25¾
Edition: 20; 2 printer's proofs, 3
artist's proofs, 9 Tamarind
impressions, 1 presentation proof
Printer: John Dowell, Jr.

51. UNTITLED (Tamarind No. 828)
Lithograph, 17 x 12½
Edition: 20; 2 printer's proofs, 2
trial proofs, 2 artist's proofs, 9
Tamarind impressions
Printer: Aris Koutroulis

52. UNTITLED (Tamarind No. 829)
Lithograph in gray and black,
14½ x 30
Edition: 20; 2 printer's proofs, 1
artist's proof, 9 Tamarind
impressions
Printer: Aris Koutroulis

53. UNTITLED (Tamarind No. 830)
Lithograph in orange and black,
37 x 25½
Edition: 20; 2 printer's proofs, 1
trial proof, 3 artist's proofs, 9
Tamarind impressions, 1
presentation proof
Note: Printed from one stone and
one zinc plate
Black-and-white edition (designated
Tamarind No. 830A): 27;
1 printer's proof, 2 artist's proofs,
9 Tamarind impressions, 2
presentation proofs
Printer: Ken Tyler

54. UNTITLED (Tamarind No. 832)
Lithograph in olive green and
blue-black, 22¼ x 17½
Edition: 20; 2 printer's proofs, 9
Tamarind impressions
Printer: Aris Koutroulis
Note: Printed from one stone and
one zinc plate

55. UNTITLED (Tamarind No. 833)
Lithograph, 36½ x 25½
Edition: 20; 2 printer's proofs, 2
trial proofs, 3 artist's proofs, 9
Tamarind impressions
Printer: Aris Koutroulis

1965

56. BEING ONE
Etching, 23½ x 17½
Edition: 20; 4 artist's proofs
Printer: Emiliano Sironi

57. CAT
Etching, 17½ x 11½
Edition: 40; 3 trial proofs, 4 artist's
proofs
Printer: Emiliano Sironi

58. DAWNLIGHT
Lithograph in gray and black,
20¾ x 25
Edition: 8; 4 artist's proofs
Printer: Irwin Hollander

59. INNERVIEW
Lithograph, 22 x 30
Edition: 15; 4 artist's proofs
Printer: Irwin Hollander

60. NIGHT SCENE
Etching, 9½ x 4⅞
Edition: 20; 4 artist's proofs
Printer: Emiliano Sironi

61. NIGHT TREE
Etching, 11⅝ x 5⅝
Edition: 20; 4 artist's proofs
Printer: Emiliano Sironi

62. NIGHT TREE ONE
Etching, 7¼ x 10⅛
Edition: 16; 4 artist's proofs
Printer: Emiliano Sironi

63. NIGHT TREE TWO
Etching, 7¾ x 11½
Edition: 40; 4 artist's proofs
Printer: Emiliano Sironi

64. REFLECTED CATHEDRAL
Etching, 8¾ x 17⅜
Edition: 40; 4 artist's proofs
Printer: Emiliano Sironi

65. REFLECTIONS
Etching, 11½ x 8¾
Edition: 40; 4 artist's proofs
Printer: Emiliano Sironi

66. TOTEM'S PRESENTS
Etching, 23½ x 17¼
Edition: 20; 4 artist's proofs
Printer: Emiliano Sironi

67. UNTITLED
Etching, 10¼ x 7¼
Edition: 40; 4 artist's proofs
Printer: Emiliano Sironi

68. UNTITLED
Etching, 17⅝ x 11½
Edition: 40; 4 artist's proofs
Printer: Emiliano Sironi

DRAWINGS

*All drawings listed are in the collection of
The Brooklyn Museum and are a gift of
Louise Nevelson in memory of Theodore
Haseltine.*

69. ARCHAIC HEAD, n.d.
Pencil on wove paper, 12 x 16½
Signed "Nevelson" in pencil, lower
right

70. HEAD (Portrait of Theodore
Haseltine), 1961
Ink on wove paper, 11 x 8½
Signed "Nevelson 1961" in ink,
upper left
Dedication: "To Ted with Love,"
upper right

71. SEATED FEMALE FIGURE, n.d.
Pencil on tan wove paper, 17¼ x 12
Signed "Nevelson" in pencil, upper
left

72. SEATED FIGURE, n.d.
Pencil on wove paper, 16¾ x 13¾
Signed "Nevelson" in pencil, lower
center

73. STANDING FEMALE
    FIGURE, n.d.
    Pencil on wove paper, 17 x 7¼
    Signed "Nevelson" in ink, lower
    center

74. STANDING MALE FIGURE
    WITH ARMS RAISED, n.d.
    Ink on wove paper, 19¼ x 9½
    Signed "Nevelson" in ink, lower
    center

75. THREE FEMALE
    FIGURES, n.d.
    Ink on wove paper, 17½ x 11

Signed "Nevelson" in ink, lower
    right

76. THREE SEATED
    FIGURES, n.d.
    Ink on tan wove paper, 15 x 11
    Signed "Nevelson" in ink, lower
    left

77. TWO BIRDS, 1961
    Ink on wove paper, 8½ x 11
    Signed "Nevelson 1961" in ink,
    lower center
    Dedication: "To Ted with Love,"
    lower right

Photographs by Wolfgang Hartmann

PLATES

ANCIENT CITY, 1953–55 (1)

ANCIENT SCULPTURE GARDEN, 1953–55 (2)

THE KING AND QUEEN, 1953–55 (11)

MIRRORED FIGURE, 1953–55 (16)

THE SILENT ONE, 1953–55 (23)

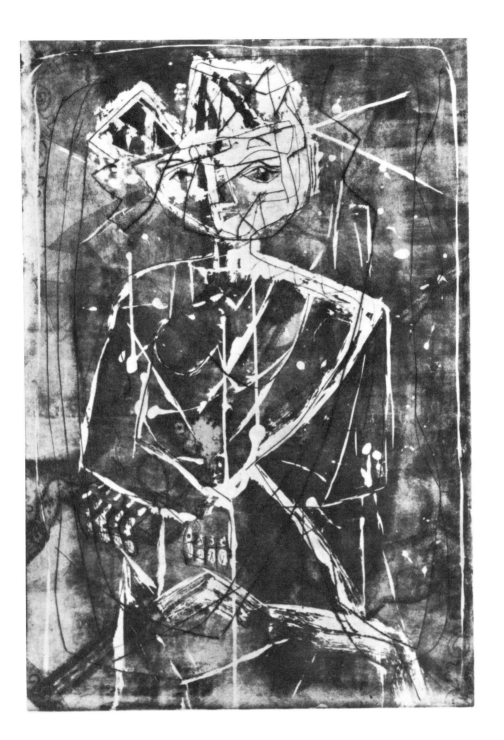

SOLID REFLECTIONS, 1953–55 (24)

THE STONE FIGURES THAT WALK IN THE NIGHT, 1953–55 (26)

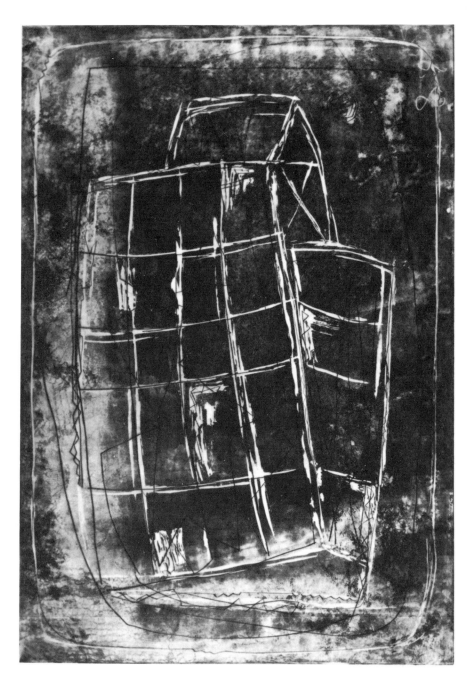

THE SUNKEN CATHEDRAL, 1953–55 (27)

THE WEST QUEEN, 1953–55 (30)

UNTITLED, 1963 (32)

UNTITLED, 1963 (39)

UNTITLED, 1963 (42)

UNTITLED, 1963 (44)

UNTITLED, 1963 (48)

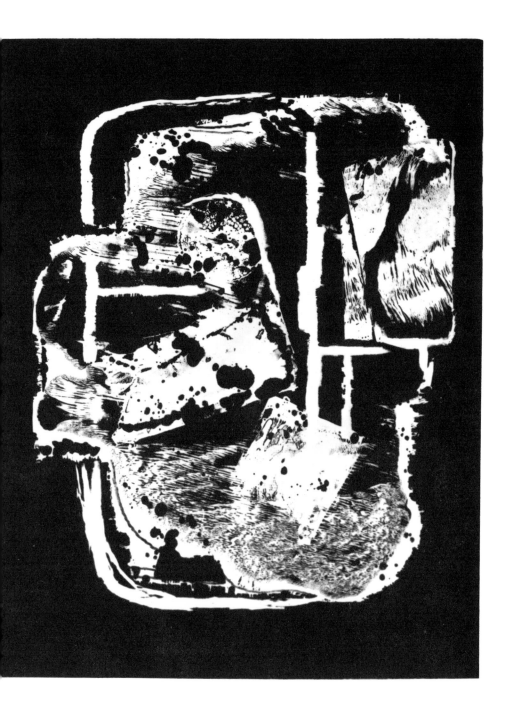

INNERVIEW, 1965 (59)

NIGHT TREE, 1965 (61)

REFLECTED CATHEDRAL, 1965 (64)

TOTEM'S PRESENTS, 1965 (66)

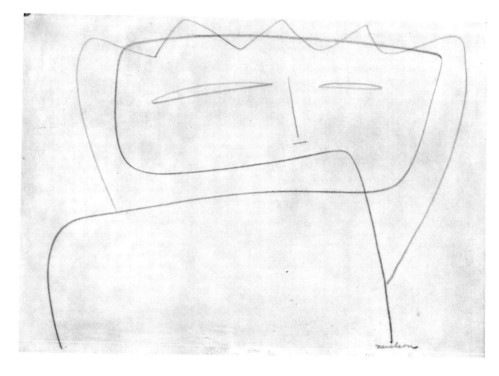

ARCHAIC HEAD, n.d. (69)

HEAD (Portrait of Theodore Haseltine), 1961 (70)

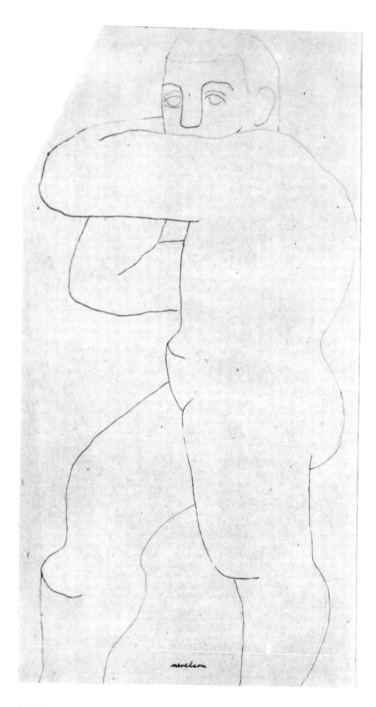

STANDING MALE FIGURE WITH ARMS RAISED, n.d. (74)

THREE FEMALE FIGURES, n.d. (75)

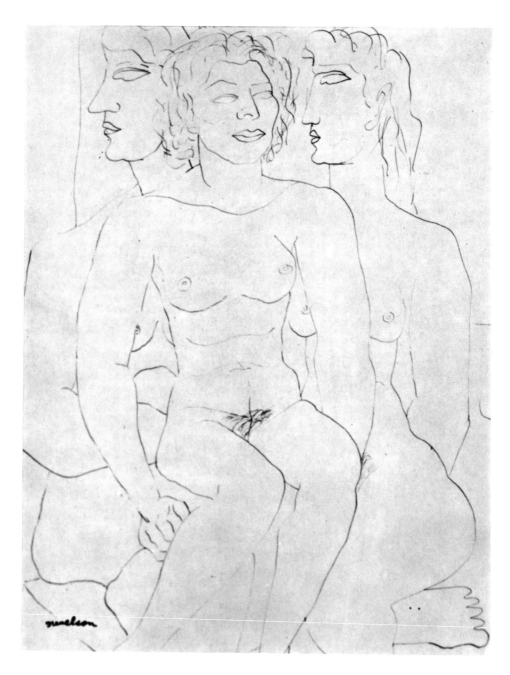

THREE SEATED FIGURES, n.d. (76)

TWO BIRDS, 1961 (77)

CHRONOLOGY

1900   Born in Kiev, Russia. Daughter of Isaac and Mina Berliawsky.

1905   Came to Rockland, Maine, with her family.

1920   Married Charles Nevelson.

1921   Son, Myron, born.

1929–30   Studied at The Art Students League, New York, with Kenneth Hayes Miller.

1931   Studied with Hans Hofmann at his academy in Munich. Worked as an actress in film productions in Munich and Vienna.

1933–36   Exhibited paintings at numerous New York galleries, The Brooklyn Museum and the Springfield Museum, Springfield, Massachusetts.

1936   Sculpture first exhibited at A.C.A. Gallery, New York. Taught sculpture on WPA Art Project.

1941   First one-man exhibition of sculpture at Nierendorf Gallery, New York.

1942–46   Several one-man exhibitions in New York.

1948–49   Archeological trips to Central and South America.

1953   Studied printmaking at Atelier 17, New York, with Leo Katz.

1954   First one-man exhibition of etchings, "Moonscapes," at Lotte Jacobi Gallery, New York. Active in artists' organizations. First Vice-President of Federation of Modern Painters and Sculptors.

1962   Selected to represent the United States at the 31st Venice Biennale.

1963   Elected President of Artists Equity Association, Inc.

1966   Continues to live and work at her five-floor home and studio on Spring Street, New York City.

AWARDS AND HONORS

1959   New York Coliseum, ART: USA: Grand Prize

1960   The Art Institute of Chicago, 63rd Exhibition: Logan Prize in Sculpture

1962   Selected to represent the United States at the 31st Venice Biennale,

1963   First woman elected President of Artists Equity Association.

1966   Western College for Women: Honorary Doctorate.

ONE-MAN EXHIBITIONS

1941   Nierendorf Gallery, New York

1942   Nierendorf Gallery, New York

1943   Norlyst Gallery, New York
        Nierendorf Gallery, New York

1944	Nierendorf Gallery, New York
1946	Nierendorf Gallery, New York
1954	Clapp Gallery, New York Lotte Jacobi Gallery, New York (etchings)
1955	Grand Central Moderns Gallery, New York
1956	Grand Central Moderns Gallery, New York
1957	Grand Central Moderns Gallery, New York
1958	Esther Stuttman Gallery, New York (graphics) Grand Central Moderns Gallery, New York
1959	Martha Jackson Gallery, New York
1960	David Herbert Gallery, New York Devorah Sherman Gallery, Chicago Galerie Daniel Cordier, Paris
1961	Martha Jackson Gallery, New York Galerie Daniel Cordier, Paris
1963	Sidney Janis Gallery, New York Balin-Traube, New York (etchings) Martha Jackson Gallery, New York
1965	Pace Gallery, New York

GRAPHIC WORKS IN PUBLIC COLLECTIONS

Birmingham Museum, Birmingham, Alabama

Brandeis University, Waltham, Massachusetts

The Brooklyn Museum, New York

Carnegie Institute, Pittsburgh, Pennsylvania

Farnsworth Museum of Art, Rockland, Maine

The Metropolitan Museum of Art, New York

Museum of Fine Arts, Houston, Texas

The Museum of Modern Art, New York

Newark Museum, Newark, New Jersey

New York University, New York

Queens College, New York

Riverside Museum, New York

Sara Roby Foundation, New York

Tate Gallery, London, England

University of Nebraska, Lincoln, Nebraska

Whitney Museum of American Art, New York

SELECTED BIBLIOGRAPHY

BOOKS AND PERIODICALS

Anonymous review. *The Art Digest*, XXIX, no. 7 (January 1, 1955), p. 21.

Ashton, Dore. Column, *Arts & Architecture*, LXXVIII, no. 6 (June, 1961), pp. 4–5.

Baur, John I. H. *Nature in Abstraction*. New York, 1958, p. 76.

Campbell, Lawrence. "Louise Nevelson," *Art News*, LII, no. 9 (January, 1954), pp. 69–70.

Castile, Rand. "Louise Nevelson," *Art News*, LXII, no. 8 (December, 1963), p. 14.

Kramer, Hilton. "The Sculpture of Louise Nevelson," *The Art Digest*, XXXII, no. 9 (June, 1958), pp. 26–29, ill.

Kroll, Jack. "Louise Nevelson," *Art News*, LX, no. 5 (May, 1961), p. 11.

"One Woman's World," *Time* (February 3, 1958), p. 58, ill.

Riley, Maud. "Irrepressible Nevelson," *The Art Digest*, XVII, no. 14 (April, 1943), pp. 17–18, ill.

Roberts, Colette. "L'ailleurs de Louise Nevelson," *Cahiers du Musée de Poche* (May, 1960), no. 4, pp. 76–84, ill., text in French.

Roberts, Colette. *Nevelson*. Paris, 1964, 85 pp., ill.

Rosenblum, Robert. "Louise Nevelson," *Arts Yearbook 3 Paris/New York* (1959), pp. 136–39, ill.

Ventura, Anita. "Louise Nevelson Etchings," *The Art Digest*, XXXII, no. 6 (March, 1958), p. 58.

"Weird Woodwork of Lunar World," *Life* (March 24, 1958), pp. 77–80, ill.

EXHIBITION CATALOGUES

Bern, Bern Kunsthalle. *Louise Nevelson,* 1964, ill.

Kassel, Museum Fridericianum. *Documenta III,* 1964, pp. 272-273, ill.

New York, David Herbert Gallery. *Louise Nevelson,* January 6–February 6, 1960, ill.

New York, Martha Jackson Gallery. *Nevelson,* April 19–May 20, 1961, 32 pp., ill. Foreword by Kenneth Sawyer, poem by Jean Arp, commentary by Georges Mathieu.

New York, Museum of Modern Art. *Sixteen Americans,* January, 1959, pp. 52–57, ill. Edited by Dorothy C. Miller.

Seattle, World's Fair. *Art Since 1950,* April 21–October 21, 1962, p. 77, ill. Introduction by Sam Hunter.

Venice, Biennale Internazionale d'Arte, June 16–October 7, 1962, p. 224, ill.

Zurich, Gimpel Hanover Galerie. *Louise Nevelson,* 1964, ill.

WRITINGS BY LOUISE NEVELSON

Untitled poem, *Art News*, LX (September, 1961), p. 45.

"A Fairy Tale," in Roberts, *Nevelson* (see above).